The Simple Little Vegan Slow Cooker

by Michelle A. Rivera

Book Publishing Company
Summertown, Tennessee

© 2005 Michelle A. Rivera

Cover design: Warren Jefferson
Cover art: Vicki Smith (art@goes.com)
Interior design: Gwynelle Dismukes
Some images © 2003-2005 www.clipart.com

Published in the United States by
Book Publishing Company
P.O. Box 99
Summertown, TN 38483
1-888-260-8458

Printed in Canada

ISBN10 1-57067-171-0
IISBN13 978-1-57067-171-5

13 12 11 10 09 08 07 06   9 8 7 6 5 4 3 2

Rivera, Michelle A.
  The simple little vegan slow cooker / by Michelle A. Rivera.
      p. cm.
  Includes index.
  ISBN 1-57067-171-0
  1. Vegan cookery. 2. Electric cookery, Slow. 3. Cookery, International. I. Title.

  TX837.R54 2005   641.5'636--dc22

                                    2005000561

Printed on recycled paper

The Book Publishing Co. is committed to preserving ancient forests and natural resources. We have elected to print this title with Transcontinental Printing on Apollo Offset, which is 30% postconsumer recycled and processed chlorine free. As a result of our paper choice, we have saved the following natural resources:

BOOK
PUBLISHING
COMPANY

11 trees
489 lbs solid waste
4,435 gallons of water
960 lbs of greenhouse gases
1,784 kw hours of electricity

We are a member of Green Press Initiative. For more information about Green Press Initiative visit:
www.greenpressinitiative.org

For
John

CONTENTS

Acknowledgments

Many thanks to my editors Cynthia Holzapfel and Jo Stepaniak for all their help and mentorship during the process of writing a cookbook, to my friend Stephanie Linton who has embarked on the vegan lifestyle journey along with me, and to all my vegan and vegetarian friends who teach and mentor me along the way, especially Wayne Pacelle, Susan Roghair, John Goodwin, and Angie Greico. Special thanks to Neal Barnard, MD, for his kindness in helping with this project and for all he does for the animals. As always, my loving gratitude goes to my husband John and sons Toby and Jay for being such good sports with trying new recipes and giving lots of gentle suggestions for improvement.

Foreword

Everyone is trying out new ways of eating these days. Some hope to knock off a few pounds. Others want to cut their cholesterol. Many of us just want to branch out and try new tastes and new products.

Of all the food trends that have burst into the public consciousness in recent decades, by far the most exciting is the explosive popularity of vegetarian dining. Just take a look in any bookstore. Twenty years ago, there were perhaps two or three vegetarian cookbooks. Today, you'll see shelf after shelf of them, addressing every possible need or interest.

Health food stores have seen a similar phenomenon. They once were tiny places with dusty shelves selling powdered soymilk, veggie burger mix, and a modest selection of vegetables. Today, health food stores are huge, featuring the most beautiful fruits and vegetables, along with an extensive assortment of substitutes for bologna, turkey, chicken, and hot dogs, not to mention at least two dozen varieties of soymilk, rice milk, and almond milk, and endless frozen desserts.

There's a reason why. Vegetarian diets are powerful defenders of health. They trim your waistline, boost your energy, and cut your risk of cancer, diabetes, or other serious illnesses. They can even reverse existing heart disease. People with arthritis often go vegetarian and find their symptoms improve or might even disappear. In our research studies at the Physicians Committee for Responsible Medicine, we have seen how people struggling with diabetes, hypertension, and chronic weight problems have finally found a diet that helps them regain their health. And, needless to say, vegetarian diets are the only choice for anyone concerned about animals or the environment.

Of the many varieties of vegetarian diets, vegan diets are the best of all. Now, some imagine such diets to be limited and Spartan. But the fact is, they are precisely the opposite. They open the door to a new world of wonderful food.

When I was a child growing up in Fargo, North Dakota, we ate pretty much the same thing every day: roast beef, baked potatoes, and corn. Or, for special occasions, roast beef, baked potatoes, and peas. I began my dietary transition in medical school, and I soon found out what I had been missing. Italian restaurants offered minestrone, angel hair pasta with Italian tomatoes and fresh basil, and sautéed broccoli or spinach. Mexican restaurants cooked up spicy bean burritos with salsa, jalapeños, and guacamole. Chinese, Thai, and Indian restaurants offered tastes I had never experienced in North Dakota. Japanese chefs made vegetable sushi using carrots, cucumbers, tofu, or avocados. In Washington, D.C., where I now live, Ethiopian, Vietnamese, and Middle Eastern restaurants offer an amazing culinary experience that made my roast beef, baked potato, and corn seem pretty pedestrian. Vegetarian foods are an integral part of all these cuisines. Even fast-food places have learned the v-word, offering veggie burgers, bean burritos, salad bars, and baked potato bars.

Which brings me to why I love this book. It shows how to have the best of all possible worlds: wonderfully healthful food designed to delight your taste buds, but with minimal preparation and effort.

We want it easy, and this book delivers. To a doctor, of course, these recipes are the perfect prescription, because they put healthful eating within everyone's reach. But even if you're not looking for better health—you just want a delicious meal that is a snap to prepare—this book gives you the tools you need.

Page through the wealth of choices, pick out one or two to get started, and dig in. I hope you enjoy it, and I wish you the very best of health!

Neal D. Barnard, MD
President, Physicians Committee for Responsible Medicine
Washington, DC

Introduction

Crockery cooking is back! Modern cooks have discovered how to save time in the kitchen by dusting off that old slow cooker from the seventies (or buying a new one) and savoring the tantalizing aromas of healthful, home-cooked meals prepared with ease.

Crockery cookery naturally lends itself to hearty stews, soups, chowders, and casseroles. Served as entrées with a crusty bread and perhaps a light salad, they can make a satisfying and nutritious meal.

While vegetarians appreciate the benefits of a plant-based diet, others who want to adopt a healthier eating style know that incorporating more plant foods is a smart way to go. Fortunately, using a slow cooker makes integrating vegetables, legumes (peas, beans, and lentils), whole grains, and fruits into our daily diets effortless and delicious.

Most cooks know that overcooking vegetables can leave them limp, flavorless, and unappetizing. As a result, vegetable lovers have shied away from experimenting with slow cookers. Fear no more! Here is a cookbook designed for everyone who wants to eat more healthfully, save time in the kitchen, and come home to a hot, nutritious meal after a long day at work or play. All that's left to figure out is what you'll do with the extra time you'll save in the kitchen!

This book is organized into sections according to epicurean favorites from around the world. My Viking heritage has given me a sense of adventure and a lust for learning about new cultures, and the Irish in me loves to celebrate. I have combined the two to bring you a world of flavorful delights. Vær så god! (Norwegian for "good appetite!") Let's get cooking!

Michelle Rivera
Jupiter, Florida

Choosing a Slow Cooker

Slow cookers first hit the market over thirty years ago and have come a long way from the cute floral exteriors and clunky designs so popular in decades gone by. There are many slow cookers on the market. "Crock-Pot" is the trade name used by Rival that has become synonymous with slow cookers in general. Other names you might hear for them are "crockery cookers," "bean pots," or "stock pots." Rival and many other manufacturers—such as Farberware, West Bend, Proctor-Silex, Hamilton Beach, and Salton Maxim—offer dependable slow cookers in a wide variety of shapes, sizes, colors, and features. Here are a few important points to consider if you are in the market for a new slow cooker.

PRICE

Standard slow cookers with minimal bells and whistles start at around $10 and can go as high as $40. Full-featured models with computerized settings for time and temperature can sell for $80 and up. Often you can find good quality, high-end slow cookers online at eBay or Amazon, usually at greatly reduced prices. From time to time I see used slow cookers in thrift stores or at garage sales. I caution against purchasing one from these sources because there is no way to know its history and whether the previous owners took good care of the cooker or adhered to the manufacturer's instructions not to immerse the unit in water. If the internal wires have been directly exposed to water, their integrity could be compromised. Since we tend to use our slow cookers when we are not at home to monitor them, it is best to avoid buying cookers from unreliable sources, as they could potentially be a fire hazard.

Size

To choose the best slow cooker for your needs, determine the capacity of food the cooker must hold based on the number of people you regularly serve and the volume of food you generally prepare. A large cooker can easily handle small quantities without any adjustment of the cooking times called for in a recipe. A cooker that is too small, however, will limit the recipes you can cook in it, and if you need to scale down recipes so they can fit in your cooker, the cooking times may no longer be accurate. If you are only able to purchase a single cooker, one with a large capacity will be the most versatile. If you are able to purchase two cookers, a larger one that holds 4.5 to 6.5 quarts and a smaller one that holds 1.5 to 4 quarts (or a "mini" that holds 1 to 1.5 quarts) will come in handy.

Useful Features

• A removable insert makes cleanup much easier. Some inserts can also double as a serving dish; and since they hold the heat well, they will help to keep the food warm at the table.

• A glass top lets the cook check the status of the food without lifting the lid, which can allow heat to escape.

• A programmable setting that lowers the cooking temperature after a predetermined number of hours is especially useful when working with vegetables. Foods kept on the warm setting rather than on high will hold their flavor, texture, and appeal a little longer.

Crockery Cooking Tidbits

COOKING TIMES

Most of the recipes in this book call for 6 to 8 hours of cooking time. This is very useful for those of us who are out of the house from early morning until dinnertime. However, many of the recipes will be fully cooked in approximately 2 to 3 hours, and some may be ready even sooner than that. Nevertheless, leaving food in the slow cooker for the day will not diminish its flavor or texture. The beauty of a slow cooker is that it not only cooks your food without tending, it also keeps it piping hot until you are ready to serve it.

MEAT AND DAIRY ALTERNATIVES

This is a great time to be a vegan or vegetarian! Those who came before us did not have the wonderful meat and dairy alternatives that are available to us today; they had to improvise their own solutions or simply do without. Fortunately, options are now flourishing in the marketplace. Dairy-free milk products run the gamut from rice milk and soymilk to coffee creamers, vegan "cheese," puddings, and frozen desserts. High-protein, healthful meat alternatives include veggie burgers and dogs, burger crumbles and "ground round," loaves, roasts, links, and deli slices to suit every taste and need. I make abundant use of these nutritious foods in a wide range of my slow cooker recipes. This is because they are convenient, quick to prepare, hearty, satisfying, and generally quite low in fat.

Not all of the meat and dairy alternatives in stores are vegan (that is, completely free of animal products). If this is important to you, read product labels closely and check for animal-based ingredients such as gelatin, whey (the watery by-product of cheese making), and casein or caseinate (a milk protein that helps soy cheese "stretch" and melt). Some manufacturers label their products as vegan, which can be extremely helpful to consumers. If a package is labeled "vegetarian," however, the product may contain dairy or egg derivatives. It is a good idea to read labels regardless, as sometimes manufacturers change their recipes or ingredients and don't indicate this clearly on the packaging.

So What Exactly Is Tofu?

Although relatively new to the West, tofu made its first appearance in 200 BC in China. Tofu has a soft, almost cheesy texture created by curdling hot soymilk with a coagulant. A variety of agents are used to curdle the milk; these include nigari (a compound found in seawater), calcium salts (which give tofu an added calcium boost), and acidic foods such as lemon juice or vinegar. The curds are then drained and pressed into a solid block.

I like to freeze and thaw tofu before using it, because freezing gives tofu a chewy, spongy texture. Simply place the unopened package of tofu in the freezer until it is frozen solid; then allow it to thaw in the refrigerator. Drain it well and press it firmly between the palms of your hands to extract excess moisture before using it in recipes. Frozen tofu will turn an off-white to yellowish-brown color; this is perfectly normal and safe. If you are not using the tofu immediately after thawing, drain the water, cover the tofu with fresh water, and store it in the refrigerator. Drain the water daily and again cover the tofu with fresh water. Stored in this fashion, tofu will stay fresh for up to one week.

Beans: Dried or Canned?

If a recipe calls for beans, feel free to use either canned or dried beans. Canned beans are tasty, nutritious, and convenient to use. If you are watching your sodium intake, rinse canned beans well before using them, as this will remove much of the added salt.

If using dried beans, you will need to prepare them a day in advance. Dried beans must be picked over and sorted through carefully to remove any foreign objects, such as small stones or bits of twigs. Place the sorted beans in a colander and rinse them well to remove any dirt or dust. Transfer the rinsed beans to a large pot and cover them with water (the water

A type of toxin called lectin is present to a greater or lesser degree in all dried beans, with its highest concentration in red kidney beans. This toxin is rendered harmless when heated above 180 degrees for at least 10 minutes. Most beans are simmered above 180 degrees for an extended period of time in order to make them tender enough to be palatable. Since some settings on slow cookers will not allow the temperature of the food to reach a simmer, always be sure to cook beans on the highest setting and check to see that the beans come to a simmer. Beans are fully cooked when they are very soft and tender. When cool, they should be soft enough to be easily mashed against the roof of your mouth with your tongue.

should reach at least one or two inches above the beans) to begin the soaking process. Dried beans should be soaked for 8 to 12 hours before being cooked. After soaking, drain the beans, cover them with fresh water, and either boil them for at least 10 minutes before adding them to the slow cooker or be sure to cook them in the cooker on high the entire time. (The beans should come to a simmer and remain there.)

Vegetable Soup Stock

Because of its reputation for being healthful and healing, and because of its delicious flavor, 1 like to use miso (fermented soybean paste) as a base for most of my soups. But if you prefer, vegetable bouillon cubes or homemade vegetable stock (see the recipe on the facing page) may be used instead. Homemade vegetable stock may be frozen in small quantities for ease and convenience. Some people like to freeze vegetable stock in ice cube trays and simply pop out a few frozen cubes to add directly to recipes.

Vegetable Soup Stock

8 cups water

2 tablespoons olive oil

3 whole carrots, cut to fit in the slow cooker

3 celery stalks, cut to fit in the slow cooker

1 small onion, sliced

1 turnip, diced

2 small red potatoes, cubed (scrub but do not peel)

1 parsnip, diced

5 slices fresh gingerroot

3 garlic cloves, coarsely chopped

2 teaspoons dried thyme

2 teaspoons dried rosemary

6–8 sprigs fresh parsley

2–3 bay leaves

1 teaspoon salt

1 teaspoon pepper

Combine all the ingredients in a slow cooker. Cook on low for 8–10 hours. Allow to cool for 1 hour. Remove the vegetables with a slotted spoon and discard (or serve them over wide noodles for a tasty meal). Reserve the stock for use in recipes calling for vegetable stock or bouillon cubes.

MAKES 8 CUPS

Using Tomato Paste

When tomato paste is used in a recipe, I also include a small amount of sugar. This is not to sweeten the finished product but to offset the acidity of the tomatoes. Purchase unsalted tomato paste, if available. This will minimize "hidden" sodium and allow you to salt the finished dish according to your preference.

Vegetables: Fresh, Frozen, or Canned?

For slow cooking, frozen and canned vegetables can be easily substituted for fresh. If you are watching your sodium intake, choose frozen vegetables instead of canned, which usually contain added salt. Frozen vegetables will also help speed meal preparation, because they are cleaned, sliced, and ready to go. Good choices include frozen sliced mushrooms, carrots, peas and carrots, broccoli and cauliflower florets, cut green beans, and onions. Frozen vegetables can be added to the slow cooker without being thawed, unless otherwise stated in the recipe instructions.

PASSIONS OF ITALY

Is there anyone who doesn't love the tastes of Italy? Move past boring spaghetti and meatballs to a festival of tempting vegetables, spices, and herbs. On the following pages is a short list of commonly-used herbs and spices for the Italian dishes found in this cookbook. The recipes call for dried herbs unless fresh herbs are specified. When adding any of the dried Italian herbs, always crush them between your fingers to release their flavor.

Fresh herbs, if available, are generally a better choice than dried because their flavor and aroma are brighter and more intense. Fresh herbs do not keep very long, however, so the best way to have access to them whenever you need them is to purchase them in small pots and grow them in your garden, on your patio, or on a windowsill.

They can be cut from the stems as needed. To replace dried herbs with fresh, use three times the amount of fresh herbs as dried herbs called for in the recipe (1 teaspoon of dried herbs equals 1 tablespoon of fresh herbs).

If your climate does not allow for year-round growing, fresh herbs can be cut in the summer and stored in the freezer. You can also gather them by the stems, tie the stems with string, and hang the herbs upside down to dry in a cool, well-ventilated place away from humidity and direct sunlight. When they are completely dry, store them in airtight containers.

BASIL is a spicy and fragrant herb that is a staple of Italian cooking. Use fresh basil whenever possible, because dried basil is not nearly as pungent and flavorful as the fresh herb. Basil can be grown easily in pots and requires very little care.

BAY LEAVES are used whole in recipes and then removed just prior to serving. Bay leaves (or bay laurel, as they are sometimes called) make a recipe smell wonderful. Bay leaves are usually not available as a fresh herb; nevertheless, the dried variety commonly found in supermarkets adds a fine flavor.

ITALIAN SEASONING is a blend of many of the dried herbs listed here. Whenever a recipe calls for Italian seasoning, you may use a pre-mixed, packaged blend, or you can mix your own using your favorite Italian herbs and spices.

OREGANO is sometimes called "wild marjoram." It is an indispensable ingredient in many Italian dishes and imparts that unmistakable Italian taste and aroma. Oregano is to Italian cooking what cilantro is to Mexican cooking—necessary.

ROSEMARY is very fragrant and is available fresh (in the produce aisle or in pots) or dried. Use it sparingly, as it tends to overpower other herbs and spices.

SAFFRON is a costly seasoning that is customarily used in Italian rice dishes, such as risotto. It is usually sold in threads and is steeped in warm water just prior to using. The result is a colorful and aromatic "tea" that can be added to the water used for boiling the rice.

SAGE is another herb that is included in Italian blends. It is as pungent and flavorful dried as it is fresh. Sage is sold whole, rubbed (crumbled), or ground. It adds a strong, spicy aroma to food as it cooks. Keep dried sage no longer than six months, as its flavor will diminish noticeably.

SWEET MARJORAM is sometimes used as a substitute for oregano. Although none of the recipes in this book specifically call for marjoram, it is found in the Italian herb blends that can be used as an alternative for the basil and/or oregano called for in many of the recipes.

THYME grows wild in the hills of Italy, but fresh thyme is usually only available in pots in North America. It serves up a powerful, savory taste and should be used sparingly. Dried thyme is almost as potent as fresh.

Buon appetito! (Italian for "good appetite!")

Marinara Sauce

2 cans (6 ounces each) unsalted tomato paste

2 cans (12 ounces each) diced tomatoes, with juice

1/2 pound zucchini (about 2 medium), cut into 4 x 1/4-inch strips

1/2 cup water

1/2 small onion, diced

1 can (4 ounces) black olives, drained and sliced

1 small jar (3.5 ounces) capers, drained

3 tablespoons chopped fresh basil, or 1 tablespoon dried

3 tablespoons olive oil

2 tablespoons sugar

2 tablespoons Italian seasoning

2 garlic cloves, minced

Combine all the ingredients in a slow cooker, and cook on low for 6–8 hours. Stir well before serving.

SERVING SIZE:
1/2 CUP
SERVES 6–8

Fresh and delicious, marinara sauce is packed with nutrients and vitamins and goes perfectly with your choice of pasta or polenta. It can also be used as a base for soups. Serve it with a tossed green salad and crusty garlic bread, and pass some vegan Parmesan at the table.

Minestrone

3 cups vegetable stock, or 3 vegetable bouillon cubes dissolved in 3 cups warm water

1 can (15 ounces) red kidney beans, drained

1 1/2 cups tomato sauce

1/2 cup sliced celery

1/2 cup fresh or frozen diced carrots

1/2 cup fresh or frozen diced onions

3 tablespoons chopped fresh basil, or 1 tablespoon dried

2 tablespoons olive oil

1 tablespoon dried oregano

1 tablespoon minced garlic

1 cup very small pasta (such as mini shells or mini elbow macaroni)

1/2 cup vegan Parmesan, optional

Combine the vegetable stock, beans, tomato sauce, celery, carrots, onions, basil, olive oil, oregano, and garlic in a slow cooker and stir well. Cook on low for 8–10 hours. About 20 minutes before serving, add the pasta and stir well. Turn the heat to high and continue cooking until the pasta is tender. Pass the vegan Parmesan at the table, if using.

SERVING SIZE:
1 CUP
SERVES 4–6

For a hearty meal, serve this tasty soup with garlic bread and a spinach salad. Try other types of beans, such as black beans, navy beans, or Great Northern beans. Minestrone is always a favorite, and its enticing aroma will make your house smell divine.

Meatless Meat Sauce

1 package (12 ounces) vegan burger crumbles

1 can (12 ounces) tomato sauce

1 cup vegetable stock, or 1 vegetable bouillon cube dissolved in 1 cup warm water

1 can (6 ounces) unsalted tomato paste

3 tablespoons minced garlic

2 tablespoons olive oil

2 tablespoons chopped fresh basil, or 2 teaspoons dried

2 tablespoons dried oregano

1 tablespoon fresh or dried rosemary

1 tablespoon sugar

Salt and pepper

Combine all the ingredients in a slow cooker, adding salt and pepper to taste. Stir well. Cook on low for 8–10 hours.

NOTE: If you prefer, 4 tablespoons ($^1/_4$ cup) Italian seasoning may be substituted for the basil, oregano, and rosemary.

SERVING SIZE:
1 CUP
SERVES 6–8

This hearty sauce gets its meaty flavor from vegan burger crumbles. Serve it over pasta or polenta.

Tomato and Garlic Soup

6 cups vegetable stock, or 6
vegetable bouillon cubes
dissolved in 6 cups warm water

1 can (15 ounces) nondairy
tomato soup

6 garlic cloves, minced

1 tablespoon dried oregano

1 tablespoon dried thyme

1 tablespoon olive oil

1–2 bay leaves

Salt

Combine all the ingredients in a slow cooker, adding salt to taste.
Cook on low for 6–8 hours. Remove the bay leaves before serving.

SERVING SIZE:
1 CUP
SERVES 6

*This delicious recipe calls for canned tomato soup for
ease in preparation. It offers a surprisingly light and
refreshing tangy taste sensation.*

SIMPLE LITTLE VEGAN SLOW COOKER

Mushroom and Parmesan Soup

4 cups vegetable stock, or 4 vegetable bouillon cubes dissolved in 4 cups warm water

1 pound sliced fresh mushrooms (about 4 cups), or 1 package (12 ounces) frozen sliced mushrooms

1 cup vegan Parmesan

2 garlic cloves, minced

2 teaspoons dried parsley

2 bay leaves

1/2 teaspoon ground sage

Salt and pepper

Combine all the ingredients in a slow cooker, adding salt and pepper to taste. Cook on low for 6–8 hours. Stir well and remove the bay leaves before serving.

SERVING SIZE:
1 CUP
SERVES 6

Serve this soup with crusty Italian or French bread and an olive oil dip. Add a tossed green salad for a satisfying meal. To make an olive oil dip, place a small amount (about three tablespoons) of olive oil in a shallow bowl. Add some fresh garlic, your favorite fresh or dried Italian herbs (such as oregano, thyme, or rosemary), a pinch of salt, and any other seasonings you like. Stir the oil to blend in the seasonings.

Cooked Veggie Salad

1 pound broccoli

1 pound cauliflower

2 green bell peppers

1 red bell pepper

1/2 red onion

2 carrots

1 yellow squash

1 zucchini

1 envelope (1.12 ounces) fajita spices

1/2 cup water

1 can (8 ounces) black olives, drained and sliced

Salt and pepper

Shredded lettuce, optional

Shredded soy cheddar, optional

Rub the sides and bottom of a slow cooker with olive oil or margarine to prevent sticking. Cut the broccoli and cauliflower into florets and discard the stalks (or add them to your next batch of homemade Vegetable Stock, page 21). Slice the green and red bell peppers and the onion into 2 x 1/2-inch strips. Slice the carrots, squash, and zucchini into 1 x 1-inch strips.

(recipe continues)

SERVING SIZE:
1 CUP
SERVES 6–8

A light citrus or balsamic vinaigrette complements this salad nicely. For an extra treat, serve the salad in a tortilla salad shell.

Dissolve the fajita spices in the $^1/_2$ cup water, and pour into the slow cooker. Add the vegetables, olives, and salt and pepper to taste. Cook on low for 6–8 hours. For an attractive presentation, serve on a bed of lettuce and sprinkle with soy cheddar.

"Sausage" and Peppers

1 pound vegan Italian-style sausage links

2 green bell peppers, cut into 2 x $^1/_2$-inch strips

1 red or yellow onion, sliced

1 cup tomato sauce or Marinara Sauce (page 27)

1 tablespoon olive oil

Vegan Parmesan for topping, optional

Place the whole sausage links, peppers, and onion in a slow cooker. Add the tomato sauce and olive oil and stir until all the ingredients are evenly coated and combined. Cook on low for 6–8 hours. Top each serving with a little vegan Parmesan, if using.

SERVING SIZE:
1 CUP
SERVES 4–6

Serve this tasty mixture over your favorite pasta or on a toasted hoagie roll.

Saffron Rice with Spring Veggies

1–2 yellow squash, julienne

1–2 zucchini, julienne

3 stalks celery, cut into $1/8$-inch slices

1 small Vidalia onion, sliced and separated into rings

1 cup frozen peas

1 cup fresh or frozen sliced mushrooms

1 cup fresh or frozen diced carrots

1 tablespoon dried sage

2 teaspoons turmeric

2 cups water

$1/2$ teaspoon saffron threads

1 cup basmati, arborio, or white rice (see note)

1 cup pine nuts, optional

Vegan Parmesan, optional

Rub the sides and bottom of a slow cooker with olive oil or margarine to prevent sticking. Combine the squash, zucchini, celery, onion, peas, mushrooms, carrots, sage, and turmeric in the slow cooker, and mix well. Cook on low for 6–8 hours.

SERVING SIZE:
1 CUP
SERVES 4

Saffron gives this rice a light yellow color, which makes a pleasing presentation with the colorful spring vegetables. Serve it with a fresh green salad or a hearty soup.

SIMPLE LITTLE VEGAN SLOW COOKER

Twenty to thirty minutes before serving, cook the rice. Place the cooked rice in a large bowl. Remove the vegetables from the slow cooker with a slotted spoon and add them to the rice. Toss gently to distribute evenly. Transfer to a large platter and sprinkle with the pine nuts and vegan Parmesan, if using.

NOTE: To cook the rice on the stove top, begin by placing the saffron threads in a measuring cup. Be sure to crumble the threads between your fingers to release their flavor and color. Add $1/2$ cup of the water and mix well to make a "tea." (This will work best if the water is warm.) Place the rice in a heavy 2-quart saucepan. Add the saffron "tea" and the remaining $1^1/2$ cups water. Stir well and cover with a tight-fitting lid. Cook on medium heat for 20–30 minutes. When the rice is tender and all the water is absorbed, fluff with fork.

To cook the rice in a microwave (my preferred method), place the rice in a 2-quart microwave dish with a tight-fitting lid. Add the water and crumble in the saffron threads. Cover and cook at 80 percent power for 20 minutes.

Pasta Primavera

1 package (10 ounces) frozen spinach, thawed

1 cup fresh or frozen diced carrots

1 cup fresh or frozen snow peas

1/2 cup white wine

1/2 cup fresh or frozen red bell pepper strips

1/2 cup fresh or frozen green bell pepper strips

1/4 cup olive oil

1/4 cup fresh or frozen diced onions

4 tablespoons nondairy margarine

8 ounces small pasta (such as shells, bowties, penne, or ziti)

Vegan Parmesan, optional

Drain the spinach and squeeze it firmly to remove excess moisture. Transfer to a slow cooker and add the carrots, snow peas, white wine, bell pepper strips, olive oil, onions, and margarine. Mix thoroughly. Cook on low for 6–8 hours. Stir well.

SERVING SIZE: 1/2 CUP (NOT INCLUDING PASTA)

SIMPLE LITTLE VEGAN SLOW COOKER

Shortly before serving, cook the pasta in boiling water until tender. Drain well and transfer to a serving bowl. Ladle the cooked vegetables over the pasta, and toss until evenly distributed. Sprinkle with vegan Parmesan, if using.

SERVES 6–8

This recipe creates a colorful and flavorful light sauce to ladle over your favorite pasta.

Eggplant Sauce over Bowtie Pasta

1 large eggplant

1 can (14 ounces) diced tomatoes, with liquid

1 cup vegetable stock, or 1 vegetable bouillon cube dissolved in 1 cup warm water

1 can (6 ounces) unsalted tomato paste

$^1/_2$ cup chopped sweet onions

$^1/_4$ cup drained capers

1 tablespoon Italian seasoning

1 tablespoon olive oil

2 garlic cloves, minced

1 pound bowtie pasta

Vegan Parmesan, optional

Prepare the eggplant 4–12 hours in advance. Cut the eggplant into $^1/_4$-inch slices. Lightly salt each slice and layer the salted slices in a colander. Lay paper towels on the top and place a heavy object (such as a water-filled gallon bottle, filled soda bottle, or heavy pot) on top of the paper towels. Place more layers of paper towels underneath the colander or place the colander on a plate or in the sink.

SERVING SIZE: 1 CUP (NOT INCLUDING PASTA)

SIMPLE LITTLE VEGAN SLOW COOKER

Let the eggplant "cure" for 4–12 hours or longer.

When ready to prepare the sauce, rinse and finely dice the eggplant and place it in a slow cooker. Add the tomatoes, vegetable stock, tomato paste, onions, capers, Italian seasoning, olive oil, and garlic. Cook on low for 6 hours.

Shortly before serving, cook the pasta in boiling water until tender. Drain well and transfer to a serving bowl. Spoon the eggplant sauce over the cooked pasta. Serve immediately. Pass vegan Parmesan at the table, if using.

SERVES 4–6

Curing the eggplant in advance helps release its bitter juices and will make the eggplant flesh more tender.

All-in-One Lasagne

2 cups tomato sauce

4–5 lasagne noodles

1 cup frozen sliced mushrooms

1 1/2 cups frozen chopped spinach (see note)

2 cups (about 12 ounces) vegan burger crumbles

2 tablespoons minced garlic

2 tablespoons Italian seasoning

Place a small amount of the tomato sauce in the bottom of a slow cooker, just enough to cover the bottom. Break the lasagne noodles into 2 or 3 pieces so that they will fit in the slow cooker. Place a layer of the broken noodles on top of the sauce. Drizzle 1 tablespoon of sauce over the noodles. Add the mushrooms. Place the second layer of broken noodles over the mushrooms. Drizzle with 1 tablespoon of sauce and half of the spinach. Add a third layer of broken noodles and 1 cup of the burger crumbles. Sprinkle with the minced garlic and Italian seasonings. Continue layering until all the ingredients are gone.

Serving size:
1 cup
Serves 3–4

Simple Little Vegan Slow Cooker

Cook on low for at least 4 hours to give the pasta time to cook. (Cooking longer than 6 hours, however, could make the pasta soggy.) The water in the frozen vegetables will help cook the pasta. You may want to separately heat a little extra tomato sauce to pass when serving the lasagne.

NOTE: If you buy frozen spinach in a bag, you will not have any trouble measuring it or fitting it into the cooker. If you buy frozen spinach in a box, you will have to partially thaw it first. If you prefer to use fresh spinach, you will need one 10-ounce bag. Rinse it well and leave the water clinging to the leaves, because it will help to cook the lasagne noodles.

You won't believe how easy this meal is to prepare, or how enticing the aromatic flavors are after it has been cooking all day. Serve it with your favorite merlot or a hearty burgundy wine and a tossed green salad. If you have a favorite cheese substitute that melts well, feel free to add it between layers.

Stuffed Peppers

1 package (16 ounces) vegan burger crumbles

1 cup tomato sauce

1 small yellow or white onion, diced

$1/4$ cup water

2 tablespoons dried oregano

2–4 garlic cloves, minced

3–4 green bell peppers

1–2 tablespoons olive oil

Shredded soy cheese of your choice, optional

Place the burger crumbles in bowl. Add the tomato sauce, onion, water, oregano, and garlic. Mix well. Cut off the tops of the green peppers. Scoop out the seeds and ribs and discard. Spoon the burger mixture into the peppers. Coat the bottom and sides of a slow cooker with the olive oil (to prevent sticking). Place the peppers upright in the cooker. Cook on low for 6–8 hours. Carefully remove the peppers from the cooker and top with your choice of shredded soy cheese, if using.

SERVING SIZE:
1 PEPPER
SERVES 3–4

Remove the cooked peppers carefully from the slow cooker, using salad tongs to keep them from tearing. Serve with extra tomato sauce and a side of your favorite pasta.

SIMPLE LITTLE VEGAN SLOW COOKER

THE COLORS OF MEXICO

Variety is the spice of life and gives us a zest for living, so get ready to enjoy the piquant provisions in this section. Mexican cooking typically includes a variety of spiced meats, cheeses, and seafood. But vegans like to experiment with south-of-the-border meals, too. So here is some festive fare to serve with your sangría and margaritas!

Unlike Italian cuisine, which employs herbs and plenty of garlic, Mexican cooking brings together a medley of spices and peppers. Here are some of the popular peppers and spicy sensations used in these recipes.

CHILI POWDER is a finely ground blend of chili peppers, cumin seeds, oregano, garlic, usually salt, and sometimes cloves or allspice. It is the primary spice in vegetarian chili dishes.

CILANTRO is the leaf of the coriander plant (ground coriander seeds are also used in Mexican cooking) and adds a light, tangy, citrus-like flavor. Cilantro is best when the leaves are fresh off the stem. Dried cilantro simply doesn't pack the same punchy flavor and aroma as the fresh leaves.

CORIANDER SEEDS are the large round seeds of the cilantro plant. They are popular in both Southwestern dishes and East Indian cuisine. Coriander has a strong, distinct scent and is most flavorful when crushed or ground before using in a recipe. Coriander seeds are available whole or ground; you can find them in the spice section of your supermarket or in ethnic specialty stores.

CUMIN is pronounced "come-in," with the emphasis on the first syllable. Alternative pronunciations include "kyoo-min" and "koo-min," also with the emphasis on the first syllable. It is sometimes referred to as "cumin fruit" or "cumin seed" and is used in many Mediterranean dishes. In the past, cumin was used medicinally to treat colic; it still is used in ayurveda (a form of holistic alternative medicine traditionally practiced in India), herbal medicine, and veterinary medicine for its carminative properties. You can purchase cumin seeds and use them whole in recipes or grind them in a spice grinder or coffee grinder as needed. Alternatively, you can purchase powdered cumin.

GREEN CHILIES are mild and sweet. Canned green chilies are roasted and peeled and are available minced, diced, or whole. They add an authentic Southwestern flavor to dishes, without the heat of jalapeño peppers. If you prefer your food extra hot and spicy, opt for the stronger jalapeños whenever a recipe calls for mild green chilies.

JALAPEÑO PEPPERS are either green or red and are fiery-hot; they are best used sparingly except by the bravest of cooks. If you are cooking with jalapeños, try freezing them first; then slice them frozen so as not to get the pungent oils on your fingers. Always be vigilant when handling them, and take care not to touch sensitive areas, such as the eyes or lips (oh yes, I learned the hard way!). Jalapeños can be added to any Mexican recipes where extra spice and fire is desired.

Enjoy your Mexican food with nondairy sour cream (either homemade or store bought, such as Soymage Vegan Sour Cream or Tofutti Sour Supreme) or Guacamole (page 60). Shredded cheddar-style soy cheese makes a tasty garnish for most of these recipes and may be added as a topping to the finished dish, since most soy cheeses don't melt very well.

Pop in a Santana CD, serve your Mexican dishes with flair, and say "Buen provecho!" (Spanish for "good appetite!")

All-Veggie All-the-Time Chili

2–4 large zucchini, diced

1 can (15 ounces) black beans, drained

1 can (15 ounces) red kidney beans, drained

1 cup tomato sauce

1 cup dark nonalcoholic stout ale, or 1 cup additional tomato sauce

1 small yellow onion, diced

1 can (4.5 ounces) mild green chilies, with liquid

4 tablespoons chili powder

3 tablespoons fresh or dried cilantro

2 tablespoons olive oil

1 small jalapeño pepper, finely chopped, optional

Soy sour cream, optional

Combine all the ingredients in a slow cooker, and mix well. Cook on low for 6–8 hours. Serve with tortilla chips and shredded soy cheddar. Top with your favorite soy sour cream, if using.

SERVING SIZE:
1 CUP
SERVES 6–8

You may replace the zucchini in this recipe with vegan burger crumbles to make a one-step meal that's higher in protein. Remember the tip for those who want to add the optional jalapeño peppers—freeze them first and handle them frozen to avoid "peppering" your fingers.

Fiesta Soup

4 cups vegetable stock, or 4 vegetable bouillon cubes dissolved in 4 cups warm water

2 cups tomato sauce

1 can (15 ounces) black beans, drained

1 cup frozen corn

1 small yellow onion, diced

$1/2$ cup chopped fresh cilantro

3 tablespoons chili powder

2 garlic cloves, minced

8–10 tortilla chips

Shredded soy cheddar, optional

Soy sour cream, optional

Combine the vegetable stock, tomato sauce, beans, corn, onion, cilantro, chili powder, and garlic in a slow cooker. Cook on low for 6–8 hours. To serve, coarsely crumble the tortilla chips and place them in the bottom of individual serving bowls. Spoon the soup over the tortilla chips. The chips will soften and expand like dumplings. Sprinkle the optional soy cheddar over the top of the soup, and garnish with a dollop of soy sour cream, if using.

SERVING SIZE:
1 CUP
SERVES 4

This is my favorite soup! The tortilla chips add a little saltiness and a surprisingly rich texture. For a complete meal, serve the soup with a tossed green salad.

Mexican Papa Stew

6–8 small red potatoes (scrub but do not peel)

1 cup water

1 pound fresh or frozen sliced mushrooms (about 4 cups)

2 cups cubed seitan

2 cans (10.5 ounces each) vegan mushroom gravy

1 cup canned or frozen peas

1 cup canned or frozen corn

1 small onion, sliced

2 stalks celery, sliced

1 tablespoon chopped fresh cilantro, or 1 teaspoon dried

2 teaspoons ground cumin

Dice the potatoes. Place them in a slow cooker and cover them with the water. Add the remaining ingredients and stir to mix well. Cook on low for 6–8 hours.

SERVING SIZE:
1 CUP
SERVES 6

In Mexico "papa" means potato. Serve this hearty stew with crusty bread or warm flour tortillas and a tossed green salad.

Black Bean Soup
with Red and Green Peppers

3 cans (15 ounces each) black beans, drained

1 cup vegetable stock, or 1 vegetable bouillon cube dissolved in 1 cup warm water

4–6 vegan sausage links, sliced

1 small onion, diced

1 red bell pepper, diced

1 green bell pepper, diced

2 tablespoons chili powder

Salt and pepper

Place half of the black beans in a slow cooker. Purée the remaining black beans in a food processor until smooth. Pour into the slow cooker and add the vegan sausage links, onion, bell peppers, chili powder, and salt and pepper to taste. Mix well. Cook on low for 6–8 hours.

SERVING SIZE:
1 CUP
SERVES 6–8

To round out your meal, serve this thick and hearty soup with fried plantains (see next page) and warm flour tortillas. Top it with Guacamole (page 60) or your favorite soy sour cream.

PLANTAINS

Plantains look a lot like bananas, but they are much bigger and starchier and cannot be eaten raw. Before they are cooked they must be peeled (like bananas). The fruit is then sliced and fried in a small amount of oil until brown and tender. Plantains are usually served with Cuban food, but they also go great with this soup.

Sopa de Veggie Mexicano

6 cups water

1 can (16 ounces) diced tomatoes, with juice

1 can (15 ounces) black beans, drained

1 onion, sliced

3 carrots, sliced

3 stalks celery, coarsely chopped

1 small zucchini, cut into 4 x $\frac{1}{4}$-inch strips

1 cup frozen peas

1 cup frozen corn

1 cup frozen soybeans

1 small green bell pepper, diced

1 can (4.5 ounces) mild green chilies, with liquid

3–4 vegetable bouillon cubes

1–2 tablespoons chopped fresh cilantro

2–3 garlic cloves, minced

1 teaspoon ground coriander

Combine all the ingredients in a slow cooker, and cook on low for 6–8 hours.

SERVING SIZE:
1 CUP
SERVES 6–8

Serve this soup with warm flour tortillas, shredded soy cheddar, and either Guacamole (page 60) or soy sour cream for an authentic Mexican lunch or dinner.

SIMPLE LITTLE VEGAN SLOW COOKER

Spanish Rice

1 1/2 cups water

1 can (15 ounces) diced tomatoes, with liquid

1 cup rice

1 cup frozen peas and carrots

1 cup frozen corn

1/2 cup chopped green bell peppers

2 stalks celery, sliced

1/4 cup fresh or frozen diced onions

3 tablespoons chopped fresh cilantro

2 tablespoons olive oil

2 tablespoons lime juice

1 teaspoon ground cumin

1 teaspoon dried rosemary

1 garlic clove, minced

Combine all the ingredients in a slow cooker, and mix well. Cook on low for 6–8 hours.

SERVING SIZE:
1/2 CUP
SERVES 4

Spanish rice is colorful, festive, and great as a side dish or entrée. Use white rice for the best results. The tomato sauce turns the rice a rich orange color, making a pretty backdrop for the myriad of vegetables in this dish. Do not thaw the frozen vegetables before adding them to the cooker.

Tasty Tostadas

2 cups vegan burger crumbles

1 can (15 ounces) red kidney beans, drained

1/4 cup fresh or frozen diced onions

1/4 cup vegetable stock

1 teaspoon chili powder

1 teaspoon olive oil

1/2 teaspoon ground cumin

1/2 teaspoon dried oregano

1/2 teaspoon seeded and minced jalapeño pepper, optional (for more heat)

1 garlic clove, minced

Salt

2–4 tostada shells (6 inches in diameter)

1/2 cup shredded lettuce (such as romaine, leaf, or iceberg lettuce)

1/4 cup chopped fresh tomatoes

3 tablespoons shredded soy cheddar

1/4 cup soy sour cream

SERVING SIZE:
1 TOSTADA

This meal goes well with leftover Saffron Rice with Spring Veggies (page 34) or Spanish Rice (page 53). Tostadas can be topped with a green molé sauce, taco sauce, or your favorite salsa.

SIMPLE LITTLE VEGAN SLOW COOKER

Combine the burger crumbles, beans, onions, vegetable stock, chili powder, olive oil, cumin, oregano, optional jalapeño, garlic, and salt to taste in a slow cooker. Cook on low for 6–8 hours.

When ready to serve, preheat the oven to 350 degrees F. Place the tostada shells on a baking sheet and warm them in the oven for 3–5 minutes. Transfer the shells to a serving platter or individual plates and spread half of the hot bean mixture into each shell. Sprinkle evenly with the shredded lettuce, tomatoes, and soy cheddar. Serve with a dollop of soy sour cream.

SERVES 2–4

Easy Enchilada Roll-Ups

1 can (15 ounces) red kidney beans, drained

1 can (15 ounces) vegetarian refried beans

1 cup water

$^3/_4$ cup rice

1 can (4.5 ounces) mild green chilies, drained and diced

$^1/_2$ cup soy sour cream

3 tablespoons chili powder

6–8 flour or corn tortillas (6 inches in diameter), at room temperature

1 cup shredded soy cheddar

1 can (10 ounces) enchilada sauce

SERVING SIZE:
1 ENCHILADA

Use your favorite soy cheese, preferably one that melts well when warmed, for the best results. Either flour or corn tortillas may be used. Corn tortillas will crumble a bit; flour tortillas will hold together a little better. Either way, this dish is fabulous.

Combine the kidney beans, refried beans, water, rice, chilies, soy sour cream, and chili powder in a slow cooker and stir well. Cook on low for 6–8 hours. When ready to serve, place $1/2$ cup of the bean mixture in the center of a tortilla. Sprinkle with some of the soy cheese and roll the tortilla around the filling. Pass the enchilada sauce at the table.

VARIATION: For Easy Enchilada Casserole, layer the tortillas and hot bean mixture in a round casserole dish. Top with the enchilada sauce, sprinkle with the soy cheese, and serve.

SERVES 6–8

Enchiladas are a staple in Mexican cooking. Serve these with Fiesta Soup (page 48) and pass some spicy taco sauce or salsa. You can kick up the heat a bit by adding minced jalapeños instead of, or in addition to, the mild chilies called for in the recipe.

Tofu with Pumpkin Seed Sauce

2 cups vegetable stock,
or 2 vegetable bouillon
cubes dissolved in 2 cups
warm water

$1/2$ cup soy sour cream

1 flour tortilla, torn into
bite-size pieces

$1/4$ cup chopped onions

2 tablespoons olive oil

1 garlic clove, crushed

1 pound firm tofu, cubed

1 cup raw pumpkin seeds

$1/2$ cup canned pumpkin

1 can (4.5 ounces) mild green
chilies, drained and chopped

3–4 sprigs fresh cilantro,
leaves torn

1 teaspoon ground coriander

Salt

SERVING SIZE:
1 CUP

It's such a sweet surprise to cook with this member of the gourd family, which rarely makes an appearance except when it's carved into a funny face or baked in a pie! Serve this dish over a bed of warm rice for a rich and satisfying meal.

SIMPLE LITTLE VEGAN SLOW COOKER

Combine 1 cup of the vegetable stock and the soy sour cream, tortilla, onions, olive oil, and garlic in a food processor. Purée until smooth, and transfer to a slow cooker. Stir in the tofu cubes, pumpkin seeds, pumpkin, chilies, cilantro, coriander, and salt to taste. Stir to mix well. Cook on low for 6–8 hours.

SERVES 4

Pumpkin is an excellent source of beta-carotene, an important antioxidant. Foods that contain beta-carotene have been found to reduce the risk of certain types of cancer and offer protection against heart disease and the degenerative effects of aging. Pumpkin is rich in the minerals calcium, magnesium, and potassium. It is also a good source of vitamins C and A, folic acid, and fiber.

Guacamole

2 avocados, cut into chunks
1/4–1/2 cup diced onions
2 tablespoons lemon juice

1 garlic clove, minced
Salt and pepper

Purée the avocados in a food processor. Add the onions, lemon juice, garlic, and salt and pepper to taste. Purée again until smooth. Chill for about 1 hour prior to serving.

SERVING SIZE:
1 CUP
SERVES 6

Guacamole isn't a recipe for a slow cooker, but is a great accompaniment for many of the Mexican dishes in this section nonetheless. Use this luscious mixture also as a topping for soup, a dip for tortilla chips, or a spread for warm tortillas.

ASIAN DELIGHTS

Asian fare offers us light and fruity flavors and textures, a natural mix with tofu. Tofu is mild tasting and readily absorbs the flavor of marinades or other foods it is cooked with, making it extremely versatile. I like to freeze tofu before using it, because freezing gives it a light, spongy texture that soaks up flavors even better. Similar results can be achieved by squeezing or pressing fresh tofu to remove excess moisture. Firm, "regular" (water-packed) tofu is almost always used in crockery cooking because silken tofu is creamy rather than chewy, making it better suited for smoothies, shakes, creamy sauces, and puddings. Here are some of the secret ingredients used in Asian cooking.

BEAN THREADS, commonly called "cellophane noodles" or "glass noodles," are translucent, gossamer-like threads made from the starch of green mung beans. Bean threads are briefly soaked in hot water before they are used in most dishes, but that step is unnecessary when adding bean threads to soups or when using a slow cooker. Look for bean threads in the ethnic section of your supermarket or natural food store.

CHILI BEAN PASTE is a popular flavoring ingredient in Chinese, Thai, and Korean cooking, as well as other Asian cuisines. It is made with fermented soybeans or black beans, mild chilies, garlic, and other seasonings.

CHINESE NOODLES, also called "mein" (as in the names of the popular Chinese dishes lo mein and chow mein), can be divided into three categories. The most common and widely used are the noodles made with wheat flour. They occasionally contain eggs, so read the ingredient list on the package carefully. Wheat noodles can be either yellow or white, depending on the other ingredients. They also may be very thin, like angel hair pasta, or very thick, like fettuccine.

CELLOPHANE NOODLES are clear noodles made from ground mung bean paste. The art of making "hand-pulled" noodles in China has long been replaced by machines, but it was once a unique and respected skill that involved stretching the paste and whirling it around, much like a pizza maker does with his dough. Eventually the paste is formed and cut into long, thin noodles.

RICE NOODLES are made with rice flour, water, and salt. They range in size from thin and narrow to wide and thick.

GINGERROOT is the knobby, bumpy root of a plant from tropical and subtropical regions (most ginger comes from Jamaica, India, Africa, or China). Although powdered ginger is widely available, fresh ginger is much more desirable for the kick it gives to recipes. Fresh gingerroot will keep well for a few weeks in the refrigerator; just slice off the papery brown skin to get to the pale yellow flesh inside. Gingerroot has long been used medicinally for stomach ailments and is a popular ingredient in a wide range of Asian dishes.

MISO, also called "bean paste," is another staple of Japanese cooking. It is made from fermented soybeans, chickpeas, or other beans, and sometimes grains, such as rice or barley. Miso can be used to season soups, marinades, dips, salad dressings, or sauces, and it comes in a range of colors and tastes, from light and sweet to dark and salty. The best misos are aged for a minimum of one to three years and contain active enzymes, which help make miso so easy to digest. Miso should always be kept refrigerated in an airtight container. Stored this way it will keep for at least a year. The recipes in this book that call for miso soup can be made with the dry soup powder that is sold in most grocery stores; it is commonly available in boxes containing 16-ounce envelopes. Just rehydrate the soup according to the package directions when you are ready to use it. Alternatively, you can make your own miso soup and use it in the recipes.

SEITAN is a delicious "wheat meat" made from gluten, a protein in wheat. It is favored by vegans and vegetarians everywhere for its versatility and chewy texture. You can purchase seitan already flavored with barbecue, teriyaki, or garlic seasonings; or you can buy it plain and add your own special touches. Seitan freezes well with no loss in taste or texture, so it's convenient to always have on hand.

SESAME SEEDS first appeared in recorded recipes as early as 3000 BC, making them an ancient and sustaining little treasure. They are commonly sold in small packets or bottles in the spice section of most supermarkets, but they are much less expensive when purchased in bulk at natural food stores. They have a high oil content and can become rancid fairly quickly, so buy only what you think you can use within three months. For longer storage, sesame seeds will stay fresh in the refrigerator for about six months, or in the freezer for up to a year.

SOBA NOODLES are flat, tan noodles that are native to Japan. They are made of buckwheat flour (soba-ko) and wheat flour (komugi-ko). Comparable to spaghetti, they can be served in hot or cold dishes. Soba noodles are wonderful tossed with a little soy sauce, sesame oil, and brown rice vinegar, and topped with a sprinkle of sesame seeds.

SOY SAUCE is a dark, salty sauce that is an essential ingredient in Asian cuisine. It is made by fermenting soybeans with roasted wheat or barley. It is used as a condiment, the same way that salt and pepper are commonly used in North America, and can be passed at the table or used in cooking. Naturally fermented soy sauce is the most flavorful; look for it in your natural food store. The soy sauce sold in most mainstream supermarkets is little more than caramel-colored water and salt.

Enjoy these Asian delights with a little warmed sake, and finish your meal with a light sorbet and vegan cookies.

Itadakimas! (Japanese transliteration for "good appetite!")

Basic Miso Soup

3 cups water

2 envelopes (16 ounces each) dry miso, or 2 tablespoons fresh miso

2 green onions, finely minced

$1/2$ teaspoon sesame oil

Combine all the ingredients in a slow cooker and stir to mix well. Cook on low for 6–8 hours.

MAKES ABOUT
3 CUPS

Mushroom and Ginger Soup

1 pound fresh or frozen sliced mushrooms (about 4 cups)

4 cups miso soup or vegetable stock, or 4 vegetable bouillon cubes dissolved in 4 cups warm water

2 tablespoons grated fresh gingerroot

2 tablespoons soy sauce

2 tablespoons chili bean paste

Combine all the ingredients in a slow cooker, and cook on low for 6–8 hours.

SERVING SIZE:
1 CUP
SERVES 4

Ginger is the spicy surprise in this authentic Asian soup. Serve it with fried rice or Chinese noodles on the side for a satisfying and tasty meal.

Hot-and-Sour Soup

6 cups vegetable stock, or 6 vegetable bouillon cubes dissolved in 6 cups warm water

2 cups cubed beef-style seitan

1/2 pound firm tofu, cubed

1 can (15 ounces) baby corn, drained

1 cup frozen peas

1 can (6 ounces) bamboo shoots, drained

1 can (6 ounces) sliced water chestnuts, drained

1/4 cup rice vinegar

3 tablespoons soy sauce

2 tablespoons minced garlic

2 tablespoons red chili paste

Combine all the ingredients in a slow cooker, and cook on low for 6–8 hours.

SERVING SIZE:
1 CUP
SERVES 6–8

This traditional Asian soup is a delicious accompaniment to Vegetable Stuffed Egg Rolls (page 74) or any Asian rice dish; it also makes a hearty, stand-alone entrée.

SIMPLE LITTLE VEGAN SLOW COOKER

Firepot Crockery Stew

8 cups miso soup, homemade or reconstituted dry (see page 66)

4 cups sliced green cabbage

1 pound beef-style seitan, cubed

1 pound fresh spinach, stems removed

1/2 pound sliced fresh mushrooms, or 2 cups frozen

6 green onions, sliced

2 ounces bean threads

1/2 cup warm water

2 tablespoons soy sauce

1 tablespoon cornstarch

Crispy fried Chinese noodles, for garnish

Combine the miso soup, cabbage, seitan, spinach, mushrooms, green onions, and bean threads in a slow cooker. Cook on low for 6–8 hours. During the last 10 minutes of cooking, combine the warm water, soy sauce, and cornstarch. Add to the stew, stirring to blend well. The stew will thicken slightly. Garnish each serving with the Chinese noodles.

SERVING SIZE:
1 CUP
SERVES 6–8

A firepot stew is endlessly versatile and can be adjusted to suit your individual taste. Don't like cabbage? Omit it! Prefer your stew with broccoli? Add some! This recipe is flexible and goof-proof, so have fun with it.

Sesame Noodles with Tofu

1 pound firm tofu, cubed

2 cups miso soup, homemade or reconstituted dry (see page 66)

3 green onions, thinly sliced

2 tablespoons grated fresh gingerroot

2 tablespoons soy sauce

1 package (8 ounces) soba noodles

1–2 tablespoons toasted sesame oil, as needed

$1/2$ cup warm water

2 teaspoons cornstarch

1 small carrot, grated, optional

$1/4$ cup sesame seeds

Combine the tofu, miso soup, green onions, gingerroot, and soy sauce in a slow cooker. Cook on low for 6–8 hours. Shortly before serving, cook the soba noodles according to the package directions. Drain and toss with a small amount of the sesame oil, just enough to coat the noodles. Remove the tofu mixture from the slow cooker using a slotted spoon and set aside.

SERVING SIZE:
1 CUP

Remove 1 cup of the liquid from the slow cooker and discard (or save to add to another soup).

Dissolve the cornstarch in the $^1/_2$ cup warm water and stir into the liquid remaining in the slow cooker. Turn off the slow cooker. The mixture will thicken slightly. Return the tofu to the slow cooker and toss to coat evenly with the sauce. Ladle over the hot soba noodles and garnish with the grated carrot, if using, and sesame seeds.

SERVES 6–8

This is a multipurpose meal that can be served hot one night and cold for lunch the next day. The flavors blend beautifully for an exotic and nutritious treat.

Tangerine Tofu with Snow Peas

1 pound firm tofu, cubed

1 cup miso soup, homemade or reconstituted dry (see page 66)

1 tangerine, sectioned and seeded

1 can (8 ounces) mandarin oranges, with liquid

1 tablespoon grated fresh gingerroot

1 pound fresh or frozen snow peas

Combine the tofu and miso soup in a slow cooker. Add the tangerine sections, mandarin oranges and their liquid, gingerroot, and snow peas. Cook on low for 6–8 hours.

SERVING SIZE:
1 CUP
SERVES 4–6

Serve this succulent, eye-catching dish on a bed of brown or white rice or soba noodles. The fresh tangerine infuses the tofu with a light citrus flavor that is sure to please, especially during the hot summer months.

Ginger-Miso Coconut Rice

2 cups miso soup, homemade or reconstituted dry (see page 66)

1¹/₂ cups rice

1¹/₂ cups sliced frozen mushrooms

1 can (15 ounces) straw mushrooms

1 cup frozen peas and carrots

1 cup shredded unsweetened coconut

2 tablespoons thinly sliced fresh gingerroot

3 tablespoons sesame seeds, for garnish

Combine the miso soup, rice, frozen mushrooms, straw mushrooms, peas and carrots, coconut, and gingerroot in a slow cooker. Cook on low for 6–8 hours. Garnish each portion with the sesame seeds just before serving.

SERVING SIZE:
1 CUP
SERVES 3–4

This makes a great side dish for Vegetable Stuffed Egg Rolls (page 74) and Mushroom and Ginger Soup (page 67).

Vegetable Stuffed Egg Rolls

1 pound firm tofu, cut into small dice

1 can (16 ounces) bean sprouts, drained

2 cups thinly sliced green cabbage

1–2 carrots, minced

1/2 cup sliced fresh or frozen mushrooms

1/2 cup sliced green onions

2 tablespoons minced fresh gingerroot

1 garlic clove, minced

2 tablespoons soy sauce

2 teaspoons cornstarch

1 cup warm water

12 egg roll skins (4.5 x 5.4 inches)

Oil for frying

To make the filling, combine the tofu, bean sprouts, cabbage, carrots, mushrooms, green onions, gingerroot, and garlic in a slow cooker. Combine the soy sauce and cornstarch in a small bowl, and stir in the warm water. Add to the slow cooker, and mix well. Cook on low for 6–8 hours.

SERVING SIZE:
2 EGG ROLLS

SIMPLE LITTLE VEGAN SLOW COOKER

To prepare the egg rolls, place about 1 tablespoon of the filling on each egg roll skin and fold. Fry the egg rolls in hot vegetable oil in a frying pan or wok, seam side down first, until golden brown all over. Drain on paper towels.

NOTE: To fold an egg roll, place a heaping tablespoon of the filling mixture in the lower center of the egg roll skin. Flip the lower end up, fold in the sides, then roll.

SERVES 12

Egg rolls are always popular and make a tasty accompaniment to any of the Asian soups and rice dishes in this book. Provide a variety of dipping sauces, such as hoisin sauce, duck sauce, or hot Chinese mustard.

Garlic Veggies and Mandarin Oranges over Rice

GARLIC VEGGIES AND MANDARIN ORANGES

2 cups broccoli florets

1 1/2 cups sliced yellow squash, in 1/4-inch-thick half circles

1 1/2 cups sliced zucchini, in 1/4-inch-thick half circles

1 can (8 ounces) mandarin oranges, with liquid

1 cup baby carrots

3 tablespoons minced fresh gingerroot

2 garlic cloves, minced

To make the Garlic Veggies and Mandarin Oranges, combine all the ingredients in a slow cooker. Cook on low for 8–10 hours. Prepare the rice about 20 minutes before serving time.

SERVING SIZE: 1 CUP (NOT INCLUDING RICE)

WHITE RICE

2 cups water   **1 cup white rice**

To make the rice, place the water and rice in a medium saucepan. Do not stir. Bring to a boil and lower the heat to medium. Cover with a tight-fitting lid and cook for 20 minutes. Remove from the heat and let rest, covered, until ready to serve. Do not stir the rice during cooking, as stirring will make it sticky. Fluff with a fork when ready to serve. To serve, spoon the hot vegetables over the hot rice.

NOTE: Alternatively, the rice may be cooked in a microwave oven. Put the rice and water in a microwave-safe container with a tight-fitting lid. Place in a microwave oven and cook at 80 percent power for 20 minutes.

SERVES 4–6

An intriguing mixture of sweet and spicy, this dish can be served as a piping hot dinner or a light and cool luncheon. It's a sweet surprise of colors, textures, and flavors.

Asian Potato-Mandarin-Sesame Salad

6–8 red potatoes, cubed (scrub but do not peel)

1 pound fresh bean sprouts

1 can (6 ounces) sliced water chestnuts, drained

3 stalks celery, sliced

3 tablespoons sesame seeds

1 teaspoon sesame oil

8–10 romaine lettuce leaves, washed and torn

Soy sauce

1 can (8 ounces) mandarin oranges, drained

1 cup crispy fried Chinese noodles

Place the potatoes, bean sprouts, water chestnuts, and celery in slow cooker and cover with water. Cook on low for 6–8 hours. Drain the liquid. Add the sesame seeds and sesame oil, and stir well to coat the cooked potatoes. Arrange the potatoes on a bed of the romaine lettuce. Sprinkle with soy sauce to taste and top with the mandarin oranges and Chinese noodles.

SERVING SIZE:
1 CUP
SERVES 8–10

This unusual potato salad sits on a bed of romaine lettuce and is topped with mandarin oranges and sprinkled with soy sauce and crispy Chinese noodles. It may be served hot for a soothing fall or winter meal, or chilled for a cool summertime treat.

SIMPLE LITTLE VEGAN SLOW COOKER

Irish Epicurean Favorites

As someone who never fails to celebrate St. Patrick's Day in a big, big way, I was always disappointed with the measly offerings for vegetarians who love being Irish (or Irish people who love being vegetarian). Now we can celebrate with the best of them, using these traditional Irish recipes that have been reworked for a cruelty-free gala.

BARLEY is one of the ingredients in that other Irish staple, beer! You can purchase hulled or pearl barley in your supermarket or natural food store. Hulled barley has more fiber and minerals, since just the outer hull is removed, leaving intact the thinner, inner hull. Pearl barley is just slightly less nutritious, because the inner hull has been removed. Both types of barley make a tasty grain side dish and are a popular ingredient in soups and stews. Barley takes about an hour to cook, so it lends itself very well to crockery cooking.

CARAWAY SEEDS are the small, crescent-shaped brown seeds typically found in rye bread. They are also used to flavor sauerkraut and cabbage dishes. If you have extra caraway seeds, sprinkle them over cooked green beans or add them to salads.

POTOTOE (Irish spelling). You say pototo, I say potato! Potatoes were the mainstay of the Irish diet for centuries until the potato blight of 1845, during which millions of Irish died from starvation. Until that time, the potato was a staple food of the Irish, and it served them very well. Potatoes are rich in fiber, potassium, folic acid, iron, and vitamin C. So enjoy the multitude of recipes in this section that call for potatoes, and remember the time when there wasn't a potato to be found in all of Ireland!

Whether you're Irish or just like to wear lots of green, sláinte chugat!
(Celtic for "good appetite!")

Irish Porridge

4 cups water

1 cup steel-cut Irish oatmeal

1/2 cup brown sugar, plus additional for serving

1 tablespoon ground cinnamon, plus additional for serving

Nondairy margarine, optional

Soymilk, optional

Combine the water, oatmeal, sugar, and cinnamon in a slow cooker and stir well. Cook on low for 8–10 hours. Serve with additional brown sugar and cinnamon and the optional nondairy margarine and soymilk to taste.

SERVING SIZE:
1 CUP
SERVES 4

No time for a nourishing breakfast? Have warm, delicious porridge waiting for you in the morning and get your day off to a healthy start. Use steel-cut Irish oatmeal in this recipe. Steel-cut oats are oat groats (whole grain oats that have been cleaned, toasted, and hulled) that have been cut into two or three pieces rather than rolled. The result is a hearty, chewy texture that puts this porridge in a completely different category from the instant mush many of us have become accustomed to.

Kitty's Carrot Soup

1 bag (16 ounces) frozen, crinkle-cut carrots, thawed

2 cups plain soymilk

1 cup vegetable stock, or 1 vegetable bouillon cube dissolved in 1 cup warm water

3 tablespoons nondairy margarine

2 teaspoons powdered ginger

2 teaspoons ground nutmeg

Salt and pepper

Combine all the ingredients in a slow cooker, adding salt and pepper to taste. Cook on low for 6–8 hours. Shortly before serving, transfer half of the soup to a food processor or blender and purée until smooth. Return to the slow cooker and stir well.

SERVING SIZE:
1 CUP
SERVES 4

Me mither's name was Kitty and she was a terrible cook. But she loved to make carrot soup and foisted it on, er, no, I mean, served it to us every chance she got. Now you can share the love with your family! Serve it with traditional Irish Soda Bread (page 92) or warm scones and margarine.

Cream of Potato Soup

4 cups diced white potatoes, or
  1 1/2 cups potato flakes
  (see note)

2 cups plain soymilk

1/2 cup vegetable stock

4 green onions, sliced (about 1/4 cup)

1 tablespoon olive oil

2 teaspoons dried tarragon

Sprigs of fresh parsley, for garnish

Combine the potatoes, soymilk, vegetable stock, green onions, olive oil, and tarragon in a slow cooker, and cook on low for 8–10 hours. Shortly before serving, transfer half of the soup to a food processor or blender and purée until smooth. Return to the slow cooker and stir well. For a completely smooth consistency, purée all of the soup in batches.

NOTE: If using potato flakes, increase the soymilk to 3 cups and the vegetable stock to 1 cup. There is no need to purée the soup if using potato flakes.

SERVING SIZE:
1 CUP
SERVES 4

Garnish this thick, hearty soup with sprigs of fresh green parsley for a presentation that is sure to whet everyone's appetite.

SIMPLE LITTLE VEGAN SLOW COOKER

Mushroom-Barley Soup

4 cups vegetable stock, or 4
vegetable bouillon cubes
dissolved in 4 cups warm water

1 pound sliced fresh mushrooms
(about 4 cups), or 1 package
(12–16 ounces) frozen sliced
mushrooms

1 small onion, diced

$^1/_2$ cup pearl barley

3 tablespoons nondairy margarine

1 tablespoon fresh dill,
or 1 teaspoon dried

2 teaspoons dried basil

2 teaspoons dried thyme

1 teaspoon dried tarragon

Combine all the ingredients in a slow cooker, and cook on low for
6–8 hours.

SERVING SIZE:
1 CUP
SERVES 6–8

*Serve Mushroom-Barley Soup with Irish Soda Bread
(page 92) and Sweet Orange Carrots (page 93) for a
healthful and hearty meal.*

St. Patty's Stew

2 cups vegetable stock, or 2 vegetable bouillon cubes dissolved in 2 cups warm water

1 pound sliced fresh mushrooms (about 4 cups), or 1 package (12–16 ounces) frozen sliced mushrooms

2 cups cubed beef-style seitan

2 cans (10.5 ounces each) vegan mushroom gravy

4–5 small white potatoes, peeled and cubed

1 small yellow onion, sliced

1 cup fresh or frozen green peas

1 cup fresh or frozen cut green beans

1 cup fresh or frozen sliced carrots

2 teaspoons dried thyme

2 teaspoons dried parsley

2 teaspoons ground sage

1–2 bay leaves

1 teaspoons salt

Place the vegetable stock in a slow cooker. Add the remaining ingredients and stir well. Cook on low for 6–8 hours. Remove the bay leaves before serving.

SERVING SIZE:
1 CUP
SERVES 4–6

Serve this hearty stew with freshly baked biscuits or Irish Soda Bread (page 92) for a St. Patty's Day treat. But please, no green beer!

SIMPLE LITTLE VEGAN SLOW COOKER

Tyrone's Herbed Stuffing

2 cups herbed bread crumbs

3/4 cup vegetable stock, or 1 vegetable bouillon cube dissolved in 3/4 cup warm water

4 vegan sausage links, sliced

3 stalks celery, thinly sliced

1/2 cup nondairy margarine (1 stick) or olive oil

1/2 cup diced yellow onions

1/2 cup coarsely chopped walnuts

1/2 cup raisins

Rub the sides and bottom of a slow cooker with a little margarine or olive oil to prevent sticking. Combine all the ingredients in the slow cooker, and cook on low for 6–8 hours.

SERVING SIZE:
1/2 CUP
SERVES 6–8

County Tyrone in Northern Ireland is known for its free-range turkey farms. We don't consume turkey from Tyrone or anywhere else, but we sure like this bread stuffing that goes so well with Tofurkey and cranberry sauce. This recipe is also named for our special canine friend, Tyrone Bob, who was our pride and joy for thirteen years.

Shepherd's Pie Casserole

1 package (12 ounces) vegan burger crumbles

2 cups frozen peas and carrots

2 cans (10.5 ounces each) vegan mushroom gravy

1/2 cup fresh or frozen diced onions

1/2 cup thinly sliced celery

1/2 cup potato flakes

1 tablespoon olive oil

1 teaspoon ground sage

1 teaspoon dried thyme

3–4 cups mashed potatoes (see note next page)

Rub the sides and bottom of a slow cooker with olive oil or margarine to prevent sticking. Combine the burger crumbles, peas and carrots, 1 can of the gravy (reserve the other can of gravy to pass at the table), onions, celery, potato flakes, olive oil, sage, and thyme in a bowl, and mix well. Pour into the slow cooker. Cover with the mashed potatoes; do not stir. Cook on low for 6–8 hours.

SERVING SIZE:
1 CUP
SERVES 5

This recipe gets its name from the "pie" that the shepherds in Ireland would make by using whatever ingredients were left in the icebox after a week of a variety of meals. So, in keeping with tradition, it can be made with your favorite vegetables or whatever you have on hand.

Shortly before serving, heat the remaining can of mushroom gravy in a small saucepan. To serve, remove portions of the casserole with a spatula and pass the extra gravy at the table.

NOTE: The amount of mashed potatoes will vary depending on the size of your cooker and the quantity of food it can hold. The mashed potatoes can be made fresh, or you may use instant potato flakes or frozen mashed potatoes. To make fresh mashed potatoes, peel 6–8 small white potatoes and boil them in water to cover until tender. Drain and place them in a large bowl. Using a potato masher or hand mixer, mash the potatoes until smooth, adding small amounts of soymilk and nondairy margarine to obtain the desired consistency. The potatoes should be smooth and creamy. Season with salt and pepper to taste. For a low-carb alternative, substitute cauliflower for the potatoes and prepare it the same way.

As with a stir-fry or curry, a potpourri of vegetables works very well. Be artistic and make this dish your own.

Caraway Cabbage Rolls

1 package (12 ounces) vegan burger crumbles

1 cup white rice

1 cup tomato sauce

1 large green onion, sliced (about $1/2$ cup)

2 tablespoons whole caraway seeds

1 head green cabbage

2 cups water

Combine the burger crumbles, rice, $1/2$ cup of the tomato sauce, green onion, and caraway seeds in a bowl, and mix well. Tear off the top layer of the cabbage leaves and discard. Cut deeply into the core at the base of the cabbage using a sharp knife. Angle the blade and cut around the core. Take out the core (this will make it easier to remove the cabbage leaves) and discard it. Carefully remove 8 or 9 leaves, one at a time, keeping them whole and intact.

SERVING SIZE: 2 ROLLS

These delicious cabbage rolls are a simple way to have a warm and satisfying dinner waiting for you after a long day at work.

SIMPLE LITTLE VEGAN SLOW COOKER

Place $1/2$ cup of the burger crumble mixture in the "bowl" of each leaf and enclose the filling by folding in the sides, then folding in the top and bottom of the cabbage leaf. Place each packet seam-side down in a slow cooker. You may need to stack the cabbage rolls depending on the size and shape of your cooker. Pour the 2 cups water over the stack of cabbage rolls. Add the remaining $1/2$ cup tomato sauce. Cover and cook on low for 6–8 hours.

SERVES 4

Irish Soda Bread

2 cups soymilk

2 teaspoons white vinegar

4$\frac{1}{4}$ cups all-purpose flour, plus additional as needed

1 cup raisins

3 tablespoons sugar

4 teaspoons baking powder

1 tablespoon whole caraway seeds

1 teaspoon salt

$\frac{1}{2}$ teaspoon baking soda

3 tablespoons nondairy margarine, melted

Preheat the oven to 350° F. Combine the soymilk and vinegar and set aside.

Place 4 cups of the flour in a large bowl. Add the raisins, sugar, baking powder, caraway seeds, salt, and baking soda. Mix well. Add the melted margarine and soured soymilk, and mix with a fork until well blended.

Sprinkle the remaining $\frac{1}{4}$ cup of flour on a board and turn out the dough. Knead until the dough is smooth, adding more flour if the dough is too sticky.

(recipe continues)

SERVING SIZE:
1 SLICE
SERVES 10–12

This time-honored recipe is a tasty accompaniment to St. Patty's Stew (page 86) or your favorite soup. For an authentically flavored Irish Soda Bread, knead the dough to two full choruses of Danny Boy (or anything by Enya).

SIMPLE LITTLE VEGAN SLOW COOKER

Lightly oil a baking sheet and dust it lightly with flour. Turn the dough onto the baking sheet, and pat it into a round loaf, about 6 inches in diameter. Using a knife with a sharp, smooth blade, cut a $^1/_2$-inch-deep cross in the top of the loaf. Bake 1 hour and 15 minutes. Transfer to a wire rack. Cool before slicing.

Sweet Orange Carrots

2 cups whole baby carrots

$^1/_4$ cup brown sugar

$^1/_4$ cup tangerine juice

1 teaspoon nondairy margarine

Combine all the ingredients in a slow cooker, and cook on low for 8–10 hours.

SERVING SIZE:
$^1/_2$ CUP
SERVES 4

This sweet and sunny side dish is a good complement to Tyrone's Herbed Stuffing (page 87) and your favorite seitan dish or meat alternative. Try using granulated brown sugar; it's slightly less sweet and doesn't cake, making it easier to measure than packed brown sugar. It also preserves the pretty orange color of the carrots instead of turning them dark.

Cranberry Applesauce

2 cups (8 ounces) cranberries

1 cup raisins or currants, optional

1 cup peeled and finely chopped apples (about 2 medium apples, any variety)

1 cup water

½ cup sugar

Combine all the ingredients in a slow cooker, and cook on high for 6–8 hours.

SERVING SIZE:
½ CUP
SERVES 4

This sweet side dish is a real crowd pleaser and makes the perfect accompaniment to Tyrone's Herbed Stuffing (page 87). It tastes great served warm, room temperature, or chilled. Because of the pectin in the berries and the apples, this sauce will jell a bit when it cools.

America's Favorites

Here are some popular national treasures, minus the animal ingredients, deliciously reworked for the slow cooker. Because the United States is a melting pot of cultures, this section includes some dishes that, while not born in the USA, have been adapted to the American palate and adopted as our own. Celebrate the joy of eating with these healthy American favorites.

NOTE: Before cooking dried lentils, inspect them for small stones or other foreign objects. This can be done easily by spreading them on a clean white plate or kitchen towel so you can clearly see and remove any dirt, debris, or damaged lentils. Before adding them to the slow cooker, place the lentils in a colander and rinse them well under cold water.

Vidalia Onion Soup

4 cups vegetable stock, or 4
vegetable bouillon cubes
dissolved in 4 cups warm water
1 large Vidalia onion, diced

1 loaf crusty French bread
1 cup vegan Parmesan or
shredded soy cheese

Pour the stock into a slow cooker. Add the diced onion and cook
on low for 6–8 hours. Shortly before serving, place a thick slice of
French bread in individual, ovenproof stoneware bowls. Ladle the
onion soup over the bread and sprinkle with the vegan Parmesan.
Place under a heated broiler for about 1 minute, until the cheese
is golden and soft. Watch closely so the cheese doesn't burn!

SERVING SIZE:
1 CUP
SERVES 4

*This soup gets its irresistible flavor from sweet Vidalia onions
that come from a little town in Georgia by the same name.*

Butternut Squash Soup

2 packages (12 ounces each) frozen winter squash, thawed

2 pears, peeled and diced, or 1¹/₂ cups drained and diced canned pears

1 cup vegetable stock, or 1 bouillon cube dissolved in 1 cup warm water

1 cup plain soymilk

3 tablespoons nondairy margarine

2 teaspoons ground nutmeg

1 teaspoon curry powder

Combine all the ingredients in a slow cooker, and mix well. Cook on low for 6–8 hours.

SERVING SIZE:
1 CUP
SERVES 8

Serve this nutritious soup when you are looking for an autumn dinner that is sure to bring warm appreciation.

"Bacon" and Lentil Soup

6 cups vegetable stock, or 6 vegetable bouillon cubes dissolved in 6 cups warm water

3 small white potatoes, peeled and diced (about 2 cups)

1 cup dried lentils (see note on page 96)

2 stalks celery, sliced

1 carrot, diced

$^1/_2$ cup chopped onions

$^1/_3$ cup chopped fresh parsley, or 2 tablespoons dried

6 slices veggie bacon, diced

3 tablespoons chopped fresh cilantro

2 tablespoons olive oil

2 tablespoons soy sauce

1–2 bay leaves

Combine all the ingredients in a slow cooker, and cook on low for 6–8 hours. Remove the bay leaves before serving.

SERVING SIZE:
1 CUP
SERVES 6

Lentils are a rich source of folate, magnesium, iron, fiber, and vitamin B$_6$. They come in a variety of colors, and any color will work well in this recipe. Serve this soup with warm bread and a cooling salad of spring greens.

America's Favorites

Corn and Lentil Soup

6 cups vegetable stock, or 6 vegetable bouillon cubes dissolved in 6 cups warm water

1 cup dried lentils (see note on page 96)

1 cup frozen corn

1 large yellow onion, sliced

3 stalks celery, sliced

3 tablespoons lime juice

2 tablespoons tomato paste

1 teaspoon turmeric

1 teaspoon ground cumin

1 teaspoon curry powder

1 teaspoon sugar

$3/4$ teaspoon ground cinnamon

Salt and pepper

Combine all the ingredients in a slow cooker, adding salt and pepper to taste. Mix well and cook on low for 6–8 hours.

SERVING SIZE: 1 CUP
SERVES 6–8

Serve this delectable soup with biscuits and a leafy green salad for a heart-healthy, low-fat meal.

SIMPLE LITTLE VEGAN SLOW COOKER

Cheesy Corn Chowder

2 cups vegetable stock, or 2
vegetable bouillon cubes
dissolved in 2 cups warm water

2 cups plain soymilk

1 teaspoon crushed red
pepper flakes

1 package (16 ounces) frozen corn

1½ cups shredded soy cheddar

Combine all the ingredients in a slow cooker, and mix well. Cook
on low for 6–8 hours.

SERVING SIZE:
1 CUP
SERVES 4–6

*Chowder is customarily served in warm, crockery-style,
single-serving bowls, with a handful of oyster crackers
on top or on the side.*

America's Favorites

Chicken-free Noodle Soup

4 cups vegetable stock, or 4 vegetable bouillon cubes dissolved in 4 cups warm water

2 vegan chicken-style cutlets, thinly sliced, or 2 cups thinly sliced chicken-style seitan

2 stalks celery, sliced

$^1/_2$ cup fresh or frozen diced carrots

$^1/_4$ cup fresh or frozen diced onions

2 teaspoons ground sage

2 teaspoons dried thyme

2 bay leaves

1 cup linguine, broken into small pieces

Combine the vegetable stock, cutlets, celery, carrots, onions, sage, thyme, and bay leaves in a slow cooker, and cook on low for 6–8 hours. About 30 minutes before serving, add the linguine to the slow cooker and stir well. Turn the cooker to high and cook for 30 minutes, or until the noodles are tender. Remove the bay leaves before serving.

SERVING SIZE:
1 CUP
SERVES 4–6

Don't wait until you are nursing a cold to enjoy this light and soothing soup.

Carrot and Black Bean Soup

2 cans (15 ounces each) black
  beans, drained

1 cup water

1 cup fresh or frozen diced carrots

1/4 cup fresh or frozen diced onions

2 tablespoons chili powder

2 tablespoons chopped fresh
  cilantro

3–4 garlic cloves, minced

OPTIONAL TOPPINGS

Diced onions

Soy sour cream

Shredded soy cheddar

Purée 1 can of the black beans in a blender or food processor. Transfer to a slow cooker and stir in the remaining can of beans, the water, carrots, onions, chili powder, cilantro, and garlic. Cook on low for 6–8 hours. Serve with the optional toppings of your choice.

SERVING SIZE:
1 CUP
SERVES 6–8

Top this soup with diced onions, shredded soy cheddar, and soy sour cream for a delectable, Cuban-inspired meal.

Miso Mulligatawny Soup

6 cups miso soup, homemade or reconstituted dry (see page 66)

2 onions, chopped

2 red potatoes, diced

2 carrots, diced

2 tomatoes, diced

2 stalks celery, chopped

1 green bell pepper, chopped

$^1/_4$ cup chopped fresh cilantro

Juice of one lime (about 2 tablespoons)

1 tablespoon turmeric

1 tablespoon ground coriander

1 teaspoon crushed red pepper flakes

Salt and pepper

Combine all the ingredients in a slow cooker, adding salt and pepper to taste. Cook on low for 6–8 hours.

SERVING SIZE:
1 CUP
SERVES 6–8

I still remember the Seinfeld episode where I first heard about this terrific soup from India.

SIMPLE LITTLE VEGAN SLOW COOKER

Tofu and Vegetable Curry

1 pound extra-firm tofu, cubed

2 cups fresh or frozen broccoli florets

1 medium onion, sliced

2–3 carrots, sliced

1 green bell pepper, sliced into strips

1 red bell pepper, sliced into strips

1 cup frozen cut green beans

1 cup sliced zucchini or yellow squash, in 1-inch rounds

1 cup fresh or frozen cauliflower florets

1 cup vegetable stock, or 1 vegetable bouillon cube dissolved in 1 cup warm water

1 tablespoon curry powder

2 teaspoons powdered ginger

2 teaspoons ground cumin

1 teaspoon salt

1/4 teaspoon cayenne, optional

Combine all the ingredients in a slow cooker, and cook on low for 6–8 hours.

SERVING SIZE:
1 CUP
SERVES 6–8

This recipe can be made with whatever vegetables you have at home. Don't like cauliflower or broccoli? Omit them, or replace them with your favorite veggies. Much like a stir-fry or shepherd's pie, this curry works well with any combination of vegetables, so be creative. You can eat this like a stew or serve it over rice or pasta.

Chicken-free Cacciatore

2 cups Marinara Sauce (page 27)
or tomato sauce

2 green bell peppers, sliced into
strips

1 small red onion, sliced

2 tablespoons olive oil

4 garlic cloves, minced

1 tablespoon dried oregano

1 tablespoon dried rosemary

4–6 vegan chicken-style cutlets
(breaded or plain)

Vegan Parmesan, optional

Combine the Marinara Sauce, bell peppers, onion, olive oil, garlic,
oregano, and rosemary in a slow cooker. Add the whole cutlets and
cook on low for 6–8 hours.

SERVING SIZE:
1 CUTLET

*Mama mia! You'll love this Americanized version of an
old Italian favorite. If you prefer, omit the oregano and
rosemary and use 2 tablespoons Italian seasoning.*

Carefully remove the cutlets from the cooker (reserve the sauce) and place them on a serving platter. Using a slotted spoon, scoop out the peppers and onion from the sauce remaining in the cooker and spoon them over the cutlets.

Serve the cutlets with your choice of pasta, topped with the sauce from the slow cooker. Pass vegan Parmesan at the table, if using.

SERVES 4–6

Chix and Gravy

1 pound sliced fresh mushrooms (about 4 cups), or 1 package (12–16 ounces) frozen sliced mushrooms

1 cup nonalcoholic dry white wine

6 slices veggie bacon, diced

3 green onions, thinly sliced

1/2 cup vegetable stock

1 small jar (3.5 ounces) capers, drained

2 tablespoons minced garlic

2 teaspoons dried basil

2 teaspoons dried parsley

2 teaspoons dried thyme

4–6 vegan chicken-style cutlets

2 tablespoons cornstarch

1/2 cup water

Combine the mushrooms, wine, veggie bacon, green onions, vegetable stock, capers, garlic, basil, parsley, and thyme in a slow cooker. Add the cutlets and cook on low for 6–8 hours.

SERVING SIZE:
1 CUTLET

SIMPLE LITTLE VEGAN SLOW COOKER

Shortly before serving, remove the cutlets from the slow cooker and arrange them on a serving platter.

Turn the slow cooker to high. Dissolve the cornstarch in the $^1/_2$ cup water and mix thoroughly. Stir into the liquid in the slow cooker. Continue stirring until the mixture thickens, making a smooth, savory gravy. Pour over the cutlets, or pass the gravy at the table.

SERVES 4–6

Serve these tasty cutlets with wide noodles or basmati rice, and pass the delicious gravy at the table.

Baked Beans with Molasses

2 cans (16 ounces each) red
kidney beans, drained

1 cup light molasses

$^1/_2$ cup diced Vidalia onions

4–6 slices veggie Canadian
bacon, diced

$^1/_2$ teaspoon powdered ginger

Rub the sides and bottom of a slow cooker with vegetable oil or margarine to prevent sticking. Combine all the ingredients in the slow cooker, and cook on low for 6–8 hours.

SERVING SIZE:
$^1/_2$ CUP
SERVES 6

Serve these beans with veggie burgers or tofu dogs, Asian Potato-Mandarin-Sesame Salad (page 78), and watermelon for dessert. Dig in and enjoy a great American feast!

SIMPLE LITTLE VEGAN SLOW COOKER

Portabella Stew

1 cup (8 ounces) soy sour cream

1 cup plain soymilk

1 can (8 ounces) vegan mushroom gravy

2 pounds portabella mushrooms, cleaned and sliced into 1-inch pieces (about 8 cups)

1 bag (16 ounces) frozen peas and carrots

2–3 stalks celery, sliced

1 tablespoon dried thyme

2 teaspoons dried sage

2 bay leaves

Salt and pepper

Combine the soy sour cream, soymilk, and mushroom gravy in a slow cooker, and mix well. Stir in the remaining ingredients, adding salt and pepper to taste. Cook on low for 6–8 hours. Remove the bay leaves before serving.

SERVING SIZE: 1 CUP
SERVES 6–8

Serve this hearty stew over wide noodles, baked potatoes, or rice. For a stroganoff dish, substitute beef-style seitan for the mushrooms.

Seitan Barbecue

2 cups cubed beef-style seitan

1 cup nonalcoholic stout beer (the darker and heartier, the better)

1 cup ketchup

1/2 cup fresh or frozen diced onions

1/4 cup nondairy margarine

1/4 cup light molasses

1/4 cup lemon juice

2 tablespoons steak sauce

Combine all the ingredients in a slow cooker, and mix well. Cook on low for 6–8 hours.

SERVING SIZE:
1 CUP
SERVES 2–4

Serve this tangy barbecue on crusty Kaiser rolls, and pass the Baked Beans with Molasses (page 110) for an authentic American meal.

Sloppy Josephines

2 pounds vegan burger crumbles

1 cup ketchup

$^1/_2$ cup fresh or frozen diced onions

$^1/_2$ cup diced green bell peppers

$^1/_2$ cup dark nonalcoholic beer

3 tablespoons brown mustard

2 tablespoons balsamic vinegar

1 tablespoon brown sugar

2 garlic cloves, minced

Combine all the ingredients in a slow cooker, and mix well. Cook on low for 6–8 hours.

SERVING SIZE: $^1/_2$ CUP
SERVES 4–6

For a quick meal that is sure to please, serve Sloppy Josephines on hamburger buns or Kaiser rolls, and pass the napkins!

Pineapple Teriyaki "Chicken"

1 cup bottled teriyaki sauce

1 can (8 ounces) diced pineapple, with juice

1 red bell pepper, sliced into strips

1 green bell pepper, sliced into strips

6–8 vegan chicken-style cutlets

Combine the teriyaki sauce, pineapple, and bell peppers in a slow cooker, and mix well. Add the cutlets whole, and cook on low for 6–8 hours.

SERVING SIZE:
1 CUTLET
SERVES 6–8

This tropical delight is delicious served on a bed of white rice or noodles.

SIMPLE LITTLE VEGAN SLOW COOKER

SLOW-COOKER DESSERTS

Have something warm and wonderful waiting for you in your slow cooker after a long day at work or play. Here you'll find recipes for: Warm Apples with Walnuts, Apples with Caramel Sauce, and Cranberry, Orange, and Walnut Compote.

Warm Apples with Walnuts

3 tablespoons nondairy margarine

2 cups peeled and diced apples (any variety)

1 cup sugar

1 cup coarsely chopped walnuts

2 teaspoons ground cinnamon

2 teaspoons ground nutmeg

Coat the bottom and sides of a slow cooker with a little of the nondairy margarine. Place the remaining margarine and all of the ingredients in the cooker, and cook on low for 6–8 hours.

SERVING SIZE: 1/2 CUP
SERVES 4–6

If you are pressed for time, you may substitute canned apples for the fresh apples in this recipe. Serve the apples warm or chilled, plain or topped with granola, soy ice cream, or nondairy whipped topping (or if you are feeling extremely decadent, try all three).

Apples with Caramel Sauce

2 cups peeled and diced apples
  (any variety)

1 cup raisins, loosely packed

$1/2$ cup vanilla soy creamer,
  or $1/2$ cup plain soy creamer
  plus 1 teaspoon vanilla extract

$1/2$ cup brown sugar

$1/2$ cup coarsely chopped pecans

1 tablespoon nondairy margarine

Combine all the ingredients in a slow cooker, and cook on low for
1–6 hours.

SERVING SIZE:
$1/2$ CUP
SERVES 4–6

*Serve this scrumptious sauce over vegan pound cake
with vanilla soy ice cream or nondairy whipped cream.*

Cranberry, Orange, and Walnut Compote

2 cups fresh cranberries

2 oranges, peeled, sectioned, and seeded

2 cups orange juice

1 1/2 cups sugar

1 cup coarsely chopped walnuts

Place the cranberries in a colander and wash thoroughly. Pick through and remove any stems. Transfer the cranberries to a slow cooker along with the oranges, orange juice, sugar, and walnuts. Cook on high for 4–6 hours. Serve warm, or chill thoroughly so the compote can thicken and jell. Stir well before serving.

SERVING SIZE:
1/2 CUP
SERVES 6–8

For a special treat, top this nutritious and colorful dessert with nondairy whipped topping or soy ice cream.

Index

A

B

Simple Little Vegan Slow Cooker